VOLUME X
CAPRA BACK-TO-BACK SERIES

Angels Burning

"Thomas Sanchez is potentially the best California writer since Steinbeck," proclaimed Robert Kirsch after twenty-five years as the *Los Angeles Times* literary critic. Esteemed poet and essayist Kenneth Rexroth went further: *"I knew Steinbeck, and think Sanchez is more sophisticated politically, more innocent at heart. Sanchez is a better writer."*

Thomas Sanchez is best known as author of the novel *Rabbit Boss,* internationally regarded as a modern California classic. ANGELS BURNING is Sanchez's moving narrative of the fateful night when the city of Santa Barbara was nearly burned to the ground, from the mountains to the sea. Originally serialized in *Esquire* magazine, ANGELS BURNING is the true drama of one man's confrontation with human frailty and nature's powerful forces, ultimately illuminating that place in human hearts which remains untamed and uncivilized, primitively open to spiritual survival.

*The Back-to-Back Series provides a showcase
for shorter literary work from both established
and newer writers and is published by*

CAPRA PRESS

POST OFFICE BOX 2068, SANTA BARBARA, CALIFORNIA 93120

THOMAS SANCHEZ

Angels Burning
Native Notes from the Land of Earthquake and Fire

Illustrated by Stephanie Sanchez

VOLUME X

CAPRA PRESS
1987

Acknowledgement is made to Melissa Mytinger and Barry Gifford
for permission to reprint lines from the book *Coyote Tantras.*

Cover design by Francine Rudesill
Designed and typeset in Garamond by Jim Cook
SANTA BARBARA, CALIFORNIA

LIBRARY OF CONGRESS CATALOGING-IN-PUBLICATION DATA
Sanchez, Thomas.
Angels burning.
(Capra back-to-back series; v. 10)
No collective t.p. Titles transcribed from individual title pages.
Texts bound together back to back and inverted.
1. Mountain life—California. 2. Coasts—California. 3. Wildfires—California.
4. Sanchez, Thomas. 5. Powell, Lawrence Clark, 1906- . 6. Malibu Region
(Calif.)—Biography. 7. Santa Barbara Region (Calif.)—Biography.
I. Powell, Lawrence Clark, 1906- . "Ocian in view." 1987.
II. Title. III. Title: "Ocian in view."
F866.S198   1987   979.4'91   87-10318
ISBN 0-88496-265-2 (pbk.)

PUBLISHED BY
CAPRA PRESS
Post Office Box 2068
Santa Barbara, California 93120

For Brothers & Sisters
David, Diana, Jeanine
who saw
   angels burning
heard
  coyotes laughing.

ANGELS BURNING

"Ho, ho, ho. You can never kill us Coyotes! We live forever."
—from "Indian Tales" by Jaime De Angulo

ANGELS BURNING

100 fires are burning their way across the splendid California landscape as I write this. Some are only brush and grass fires in the southern foothills, others rage in tall northern-most forests, more scream with a red fury totally out of control, defying everything man can pit against them, such as the blaze devouring the entire 200,000-acre Tassajara Wilderness behind Big Sur. When I was a boy in California the fear residing deep in our native souls was *earthquake,* the force capable of rising like an awakening monster, shrugging from its crusty shoulders

9

all man's feeble structures. I recall a morning when I was twelve years old in Catholic boarding school near Mission San Juan Batista, at 6 A.M. the long dormitory hall sleeping seventy boys in bunks began to tremble like the topmost limb of a redwood tree. The trembling grew to a clattering as the building shook, rattling rows of windows until the dormitory seemed a speeding boxcar hurtling on broken track. Then the force was gone, leaving only a few cracks etched along the outside stone walls, and seventy boys clutching bed covers with white-knuckled fists, convinced the jaws of earth had opened to receive them.

I have probably experienced fifty more earthquakes of such magnitude since that early dawn, mammoth groaning nudges from the bowels of the earth, reminding us on this magnificent crust at the western edge of the continent that we are here by the grace of Nature, and what Nature giveth, like the Lord, she also taketh. Earthquakes were as common to my boyhood as summer twisters in Dorothy's Kansas, or flashfloods in the mideast, or hurricanes in the southeast. All part of life, all posing unique threats to their region. Leaving people not residing there shaking knowing heads and thinking, "How in the world can those poor souls go on living with such impending doom?"

One summer, when I was a teenager, my family stopped in Fargo, North Dakota to give our overheating Buick a deserved rest before heading for the Black Hills and the four mammoth white presidential faces carved into Mount Rushmore. Much of Fargo had disappeared, treelined streets of houses ripped out in the path of a twister, ripped out and flung by demon winds across endless brown waves of the high plains. In what little

debris left stood the front wall of a building formerly housing a local business. Secured to the wall was a metal plaque informing boastfully the building had been built up from scratch after two similar disasters. Our family stood for the longest moment before that wall, shaking sad heads in disbelief. We wondered how on earth people could knowingly build in the path of such force from the summer sky hellbent on destroying them, hellbent on buying back the spirits of buffalo who once grazed by thousands where tracts of homes now sprung up. We returned to California smug with the knowledge we were a good deal more intelligent than the poor folks of Fargo. We had sense enough not to live where nature made it manifestly clear we were not welcome.

Earthquakes are such second nature to California life it never bothered me living right on top of the most potentially dangerous one of all, the one residing deep within the chasms of the San Andreas Fault. For years I lived north of San Francisco on the Point Reyes Peninsula, a mountainous finger of land running well timbered and awesomely beautiful between the Pacific Ocean and the twenty-two-mile Tomales Bay. If the Peninsula was a ship, and on that ship was a masthead facing the fate of the open ocean, that is where I lived, on a tip of land formed millions of years before. The Point Reyes Peninsula was born of a force rupturing from the ocean's floor, splitting the coast, forging the Tomales Bay, continuing south to carve the San Francisco Bay into being, throwing up an entire new range of mountains, tearing and twisting the earth's hide into a thousand knots of improbable terrain. If one surmounts Mount

Vision on the Point Reyes Peninsula, to the very top of what has been called "the Island of Time," one overlooks the Tomales Bay to the continental mainland, land millions of years younger than that beneath one's feet. Such is the force which created the astonishing coast of California. Rome was not created in a day, California was not created in a million years.

When my first novel, *Rabbit Boss,* suddenly sold as a movie, I was living on that "Island in Time," where the watery mouth of Tomales Bay yawned like a sea monster to receive furious San Andreas rifts. The gladhands of Hollywood beckoned, tugging my lichen-covered northern California soul south, into a world of tropic delights and alligator-lizard nights. I succumbed. I became a shameless palm aficionado. I tracked down elegant, brooding dragon trees in the hills of Hollywood. I would walk a mile to see a jacaranda tree's gorgeous purple smile, To witness the spearing force of cream-colored yuccas in summer bloom on steep redrocked mountains awed me, sent me scrambling into secluded corners of tight-vined, jasmine-scented gardens, chattering feverishly like a madcap monkey gone bananas under the banyon tree. In the midst of this tropic stupor I searched for a house conjured from my studies of the grand epoch of dazzling Californios on vast ranchos. I searched for the grandiose dream of first Spaniards who named this land California. Not the dream of Conquistadores, but those who walked behind, in the dust of the conquerors' thundering horses, dreaming of wide verandas looking straight to sea, of orange and olive trees cascading down mountainsides. I searched like a demon for more than half a year, driving 3,000 miles up and down the state,

chasing any lead, traveling on the slim hope of surreptitious midnight calls from real-estate sources that nirvana just came on the market.

Finally I gave up dreaming the impossible dream, headed south, below Mexico City into the silver mountains of Tasco, where bulls have fireworks for horns and ragged boys stand alongside nearly deserted roadways holding up prize offerings of four-foot iguanas by lashing tails. Then an urgent telegram. High above the town of Santa Barbara, in the Santa Ynez mountains of California, was perhaps the embodiment of the *dream*. What did I know of Santa Barbara? Big red mountains rising out of big blue sea, fabulous pink stone Mission called the queen of them all, film stars and European opera singers from the '20s speeding along palmy avenues in vintage Rolls' and Jags, and the most famous garden in the whole West, Madame Ganna Walska's Lotus Land, one square mile of botanical bliss spiked off from public view by eight-foot-high blue agave cacti, and my favorite, elegant brooding dragon trees. What I didn't know about Santa Barbara wouldn't hurt me, or so it seemed, until I discovered the truth.

The truth is Santa Barbara is a well-guarded expensive secret. The whole damn place is a private garden, courtyards rivaling those of Córdoba, a proud sense and poetic style of early southwest history clearly living at ease with the present. An old joke in Santa Barbara has it there are only two classes of people, those who can afford gardens, and those who can afford to work in them. Everyone is a fanatic of loving toil in Santa Barbara's garden of Eden. That's why when the oil burst from one of the

derricks in the Santa Barbara Channel several years back it
caught the entire world's fancy, the black primordial ooze that
greases the engine of civilization defiling the shoreline of a
gleaming, red-tiled fairytale city on the Pacific. By the time I
rolled into fairytale land the Big Oil Spill was a fading memory.
People were obsessed by an earlier catastrophe. No, not the
devastating earthquake of 1925 which brought the entire town
to its stone and adobe foundations, but the Great Coyote of '64,
when the garden of Eden become hell, and hell became a way of
life.

In Santa Barbara I hit the golden paydirt of my dream. Arriving from Taxco I stepped out of my car at one thousand feet
above sea level. Spread before me was a sight I'll never forget. I
had come home at last. Nine levels of crumbling adobe walls
thick as an ox leg were laid into the mountainside, a mirage
from the past with a town distant and gleaming far below. A
stageset really, conceived by a Shakespearean actor and daring
dreamer in the 1950s. He hired bridge builders from South
America, poets from Big Sur, engineers from New England,
cowboy polo players from Arizona to conjure and cajole the
soul of old California. The adobe bricks were made on the site,
each block sixty-five pounds, thousands of them set back into
the mountain from which they came. The massive timbers of
the Ellwood Pier were pulled from the sea and trucked up the
mountain to beam and strut over the adobe, supporting a lake
of red tile. What a house, what a casa, what a dream! But in
Santa Barbara it was "just another old house." In Santa Barbara
people have become spectacularly jaded with beauty. When the

sun is out Santa Barbarans raise their hands and smile up at clean blue sky, "Just another beautiful day." The overgrown garden of my dream house had been laid out by the former head man at the Huntington Botanical Gardens in San Marino. Why was it for sale, and at one-fifth the price it should have been going for? The answer was in the two-hundred-year-old olive orchard surrounding the Casa. The thick trunks were discolored, shakes of black veining up their sides, lingering signs of the Great Coyote. The splendid hacienda melting like a Mexican chocolate wedding cake on the mountaintop was going for a song because people still remembered, people were still scared. People knew the actor built another house, spiraling six stories up the mountain, a wood-and-glass poor man's Hearst Castle. That house was devoured by the Great Coyote in ten minutes.

The Great Coyote got its name because it started on a road pointing down a steep canyon to the sea, called "Coyote." Coyote Road took its name from earliest Spanish land grant maps showing a huge draw of land split wide open from mountain peaks without interruption to the beach. A place marked on Spanish maps "Cañada del Coyote," named for hundreds of Coyote packs which claimed the vast cañada home. Santa Barbara grew up west of Cañada del Coyote, the elegant town of Montecito grew up to the east. The cañada became the last wilderness belt on the Santa Barbara coastline, territory inhabited almost exclusively by coyotes driven from all other natural haunts. Coyotes of the cañada were marked for ultimate extinction as the gardens of Santa Barbara and Montecito marched on

them with waving palms and walls of banana leaves. But Coyote is nothing if not cunning. Matter of fact, Coyote isn't one thing, he is *all* things. California Indians regarded Coyote at once creator, trickster, liar, messiah, evil, good, and everything in between. A slippery character, no matter how you slide him. Even Coyote's voice can play tricks on you. His barking and wailing can sound like children laughing, a police siren, a man growling from hunger, or any number of unlikely things depending on his mood. It is not infrequent the Santa Barbara police receive calls about a woman being beaten somewhere in the neighborhood, actually it is Coyote howling up at the moon from the cañada.

It was no happenstance when the Great Coyote fire began in late summer of 1964, giving birth to a new fire totem. People didn't exclaim, for thirteen days and fourteen nights, the fire was burning out of control, they spoke instead of Coyote being on the rampage. Coyote became flames, fanned by ninety-mile-an-hour desert Santa Ana winds leaping over mountain peaks, establishing a forty-mile fire line, ripping up trees and tele-phone poles, hurtling them thousands of feet through the air. The flames of Coyote swirled around the outskirts of Santa Barbara, raining from the sky a black outpouring of cinders big as baseballs. Coyote raced north, south and east through rugged Los Padres National Forest, threatening to burn out nesting grounds of the last giant California condors.

When I asked why the adobe house way up on top of Cañada del Coyote was for sale the answer was always the same, "Because of Coyote." Now, I am a believer of animal totems.

We are all brothers and sisters under the skin. And I am a believer in Coyote's protean behavior, matter of fact Coyote is the closest spirit to a writer I can possibly imagine. Writers are liars and creators, saints and scoundrels, poets and pretenders. So, regardless of coyote's local reputation I bought the adobe and promptly named it Casa Coyote. Then I had a long talk with Coyote. I told him it was an outrage he was now associated only with devastating fires. I told him in the whole history of Coyote not once was it ever recorded he started a fire that harmed anyone as had Man. I told him he was always welcome in the oasis of my garden. He had an open invitation every night to hang around and sing up the moon. I gave him what he most coveted, a perennial dripping faucet in the olive orchard where he could count on a thirst-quenching lick or two. I even placed a four-foot clay sign in the ground, declaring *Casa Coyote*. I had stationery made with Coyote singing to the night across the letterhead. Some nights, when I heard him singing up the moon from the cañada like a forlorn lover or drunk cowboy, I would step out onto the veranda, throw back my head and howl. Then there would be dead silence, until he returned my song with a better one of his own, a glamorous existential tune that made me feel right at home. No doubt about it, I took my totem seriously and for keeps. I knew I had chosen well, but not how well until the beginning of what started as, "The Second Great Coyote fire."

Only weeks before the second great fire in Santa Barbara within thirteen years I returned to Casa Coyote from a long winter holed up in the Rocky Mountains writing a new novel. Because of a devastating drought I knew the fire season would begin early in California. My brother, a lumberjack in the Sierra Nevada Mountains, came down to help clear a firebreak around the Casa. We were aided by a crazy Frenchman who talks to birds, and has fought the six major fires in Santa Barbara over the past twenty years. The Frenchman joined us, with a crew of what Californians charmingly refer to as "illegal aliens from south of the border," and immediately started hacking through thick sage and clumps of yucca. The night before the fire my wife unexpectedly flew in from London, where she was searching for a place for us to live, announcing there was no more beautiful place on earth than Santa Barbara. She had felt an overwhelming sensation to immediately return, certainly a premonition. The day of the fire I celebrated my daughter's homecoming from England, buying six white doves, placing

them in an aviary until they learned to trust us and could be set free to fly about the garden.

Seven o'clock that evening we were sitting at an outdoor cafe downtown. A siren sounded in the background of our meal. A big pumper-truck rolled by with black-helmeted firemen hanging precariously from its sides. With the sound of a second siren I went to the corner, looking high up in the mountains to Casa Coyote seven miles away. There was no smoke anywhere. But something tugged away at me; a strange sight I noticed on the way down Coyote Road only fifteen minutes earlier, a lone fireman standing before his red car, nervously shaking his fingers as if someone just rapped him across the knuckles with a cue stick. The gathering sound of sirens drowned out all possibility of talk in the cafe. I knew more than one fire-station was responding to the action. I left the table and went back to the corner. Fire trucks rolled one after another down the street in a whirring red parade, but still no smoke. I hurried up the block to the next corner and saw it. A grayish column of piling clouds swirled against the mountains at the very top of Coyote Road, exactly where the Great Coyote started thirteen years before when frisky kids playing with matches touched off a nearly unstoppable fiery rampage. I had only one thought. Get to the Casa before roads were barricaded. I knew it was already impossible to drive up Coyote Road. We took the bottom road through Conejo Pass. Sundowner winds, created by summer's long days of heat radiating back from mountain boulders as cool sea air moved in, were blowing fifty miles an hour, bending one-hundred-foot eucalyptus trees along the road nearly double.

It was clear, with sundowner winds there was no chance for what was burning to stay in one place. The main thing was not to get cut off from the Casa by police barricades, or the fire itself, since we had no idea in how many directions it was racing.

A story is told about a man who lost his house in the Great Coyote. He had been leaving the threatened house all day, stripping everything of value as balls of fire shooting along ridges in swirling half-mile jumps headed straight for his home. After his tenth trip out he drove back up to the police barricade blocking the road to his home. A sheriff's deputy stopped him. The man's house was burning, the situation too dangerous to let him pass. The man started screaming, "Come on up and help save my house, you bastards! C'mon goddamnit, let me through." There was nothing the men at the barricade could do. They had their orders, evacuate everyone from endangered areas. The man slammed the accelerator pedal to the floor, crashing through the barricade. The deputy hung onto the side of the speeding car, half running, half drawing his revolver and firing through the window, blowing the dashboard apart before the man's startled face. The man swerved the car to a dead stop. In a state of shock he was led off to jail.

Roads to Casa Coyote were still open, but never would we have succeeded in traveling up Coyote Road. The fire was already a mile-long red tongue lashing down the cañada, not more than a quarter-mile from my home. It was seven-thirty at night, five houses burned in the distance. Little did we suspect as we gained our first perspective of the ensuing holocaust from

the Casa's veranda, it would be us against the fire gods for the next twenty-four hours. The wind was coming strong, hot and deadly over the tile roof of our adobe house, headed straight toward the city and the sea. But the sundowner winds are tricky and devilish, obeying no law of course, and when they build to such blustery fury are bereft of rhyme or reason, uprooting two-hundred-year-old trees, crashing limbs onto rooftops, fanning flames three, four hundred feet high. The power of the sundowner was at the fire's back, a red tornado streaking down the deep canyon toward Santa Barbara spread white and rosy in the glow of sunset below. There was every evidence that upon the whim of a strong gust the fire could change course and advance straight for us. The thing to do was to respect it, to anticipate its sudden capricious fury. Everyone went through the house pinpointing articles of value to be saved. After the Great Coyote the Casa had been rigged and piped for another similar disaster, twenty tall rainbird sprinklers surrounded the house. It took me more than twenty minutes to test every one, aiming the spray at the possible line of attack the fire would take when the sundowner twisted back up the mountain. The sun was sinking fast, the air filled with the sound of wind and wailing sirens. Billowing clouds of smoke masked the entire sky; two borax bombers droned overhead, heading for Coyote Road to dump fire retardant loads before final darkness.

If ever there were peacetime heroes they certainly must be the bomber pilots who fight fires. In dare-devil feats of flying bravado they swoop low over burning treetops, doing battle against flaming rampage. With the support of the sundowner

winds behind it this fire was a formidable enemy. The bombers didn't stand a chance, and the pilots knew it. The air turbulence was strong enough to still the big engines, plummeting the planes into flames below. Still they came in, droning on, dipping low, suddenly pulling up to get off one last load before dark. There would be no second chance, no possible way the planes could continue to do battle until the following morning, by then the entire city of Santa Barbara might be nothing more than steaming high-class rubble.

By eight-thirty the sun was gone. Thick darkening clouds piled a thousand feet overhead. It seemed only we were left against a growing wall of flame feeding off one house after another like the devouring breath of a giant dragon. We stood on the veranda, awed and humbled. The fire was totally out of control. There was no way to stop it before morning, no telling which way it might turn its fury. All inventions of man were powerless to halt such a wanton force of nature. Suddenly I knew I was about to lose everything. Every beautiful Santa Barbara day would go up in smoke, every family photograph, every memory and special spirit invested in hundreds of artifacts we gathered through life like all other emotional human packrats. There was no escape except total loss. The fire was going to get us, a towering red curtain quickly drawing closed to end the third act. A strange and definite feeling overtook me. Who gives a damn for life's *things,* its bounty and booty, first drafts of novels, old love letters, a child's favorite toys. "Let it burn," I said to myself. "Let the whole beautiful place go to the ground. I'm not going to run around trying to salvage this and

that from a hopeless situation. I'm not going to bow down in the face of disaster, scurrying, about, grabbing what can be grabbed, stealing pieces of an old life in order to begin a new one. Let it burn is what I say!"

It was then the fire became an entity, a spirit, a robust presence to communicate with. I looked down the cañada at the curtain of flame which had split in five separate directions and shouted, "Come on up and take it then! Come and get it! If that's how it is to be, then let it be!" Talking to a fire is a primal and simple thing to do, following hard on the heels of fear and self-pity, after one has gone beyond questions like, "Why me? Why should my place burn? Why not some heavy hitter who has been having lots of luck lately, winning rich in the Big Casino of Chance?" Talking to fire is shrewd and healthy, because its flaming spirit is real and immediate, a demon of mercy come to simplify your life, a burning angel of extermination hellbent on discovering what steel sinews still exist in some forgotten part of our over-civilized souls.

Others have learned the language of fire. Various Plains Indian tribes periodically piled worldly possessions into a lodge, invited the fire spirit in, talked to him cordially, joked with him, shed a tear with him, then put a torch to the whole place. Other peoples burned their dead, talking like crazy to the flames, asking very personal favors. Many California Indians started fires, to drive game out from forests, to cleanse the earth, to explode seeds from cones which can only germinate during an inferno. After these fires deer rolled in the ashes to remove bloodsucking ticks, and life-giving grasses sprang up. So I got to

talking away at the fire from the vine-covered veranda, blustering on like a wounded baboon, defying the flames to come up and snuff me out. Besides, what does one save from a lifetime of mementos? I used to ask my college students during the combative days of the '60s, "If America was a burning house, and you could save one thing from it, what would that thing be? "Freedom," said some. "My girlfriend," said several. Another told about one of the periodic Malibu fires which burn down the brown grass mountains across the Coast Highway onto the piers of the Pacific Ocean. He said blonde starlets in bikinis led skittery palomino horses down the molten asphalt highway as grown men ran about like Chicken Little, throwing hands in the air and screaming, "What should I save? What should I save?" His mother darted back into her burning house to save only one item, one sweetheart artifact, irreplaceable and dear, her son's bronzed baby shoes.

As I chatted away to the fire I also told it I would not be rebuilding after the Casa went up in an elegant puff. I was going to walk away from the pain. And as I talked I realized what a liar I was. Of course, I would rebuild, plant the scorched earth. It's a funny thing, when you are burned out of a place your instinct is to return, not to run. After you make the decision to fight a fire, and it is such an inferno steam hisses from your hose instead of life-preserving water, you become a crazed beast with a singular lust for survival, willing to let flames roar around as you drape yourself in wet blankets, dumping buckets of water over your head. You become defiant, irrational, and very human. So we filled all the bathtubs in preparation for the

water supply to drop to a dribble. We turned all the lights on, so when flames reached the Casa and smoke swirled everything to darkness there would be light enough to see. The reflection of the flames against the walls of the Casa and mountains behind were our only reality. So much so that when the electricity did go off it went unnoticed, until I saw lights from a car snaking through trees along the driveway. My friend the Goat, Noel Young, the hardheaded two-fisted publisher of Capra Press who successfully defended his own home in the Great Coyote, arrived with flashlights and candles. "This is worse than the Great Coyote," the Goat spoke sadly, gazing from the veranda at the fire tornado jumping from rooftop to rooftop, its intense heat exploding hundred-foot-high eucalyptus trees in brilliant showers of white embers. "The radio claims winds are ninety miles an hour behind those flames and there's an unconfirmed report fifteen people have already been killed. The whole thing is headed straight downtown, there's nothing to stop it except the sea."

It was time to evacuate. We piled personal belongings in the cars. I ran through the darkened house locking windows and tying doors together so advancing flames couldn't suck them open. Minutes became hours, hours became lifetimes. There was nothing to do except wait and watch which way the fickle winds of fate would blow. The curtain of flame rose higher around us, the fiery opera in full force, a hundred houses already burned. I walked out on the point of land at the bottom of the olive orchard, commanding a view deep into the cañada, high to a long table of land five hundred feet above the sea called the Riviera. Gracious villas were illuminated on the Riviera hillside in unreal light, extraordinary illumination like ethereal sunsets of Turner paintings, except it was midnight and the jaws of hell had opened. The blistering wind lashed my body with the force of a thousand heavy hands trying to slam me to earth. Standing still felt like running. Furious hot gusts slapped me in the face as I watched through tears whipping from my eyes. The fire jumped out of the deep canyon within three minutes, leaping

up onto the lush growth of the Riviera like a lion clawing onto a zebra's back. Roof after roof dazzled into flame, entire three-story homes exploding, walls billowing out in torrents of waffling heat. The wind carried distant sounds of sirens and screams, dreams going up in smoke. Swirling red lights from a fire-engine stationed protectively before a house were engulfed in waves of darkening smoke. The pumper-truck appeared again in a sudden wind shift, towering sprays of water arcing hopelessly into the surrounding wall of flame. The pumper-truck was trapped, there was no possible escape from fingers of flame roaring along the hillsides, exploding forests of sycamore and eucalyptus trees, moving like monstrous lava flows toward the city. Half of the Riviera was burning; flame, sparks and smoke cascading over the life pulse of the pumper-truck's lights. A new rain of black cinders showered from the air as I stood talking to the wind, speaking to the very Fire Gods themselves. A conversation private and desperate, my sense of utter helplessness filling the sorrow in my bones with an odd and certain sense of destiny, as if life conspired to bring me to this windy point, to contemplate devastation, to cut me loose from everything of value rooting me to the earth being scorched to some pure, originating point in creation. It is difficult to reconstruct what I said to the fire, because my heart had gone back to a distant age, to a time before language and logic of man. But I'll never forget what I said to Coyote barking and wailing through the cañada in sounds almost identical to fire-engine sirens. I asked Coyote to save me.

The flames turned from the Riviera as if suddenly remem-

bering something and headed straight for the Casa. The fire was in total control, pumper-trucks and bulldozers pulled back, an army of equipment groaning away from the ruthless inferno, coming up the cañada, forming a last line of defense on the mountain road encircling the Casa. A police car racing up the driveway stopped, two uniformed men inside rolled down their windows, every strained line in their weary faces silently attesting to a hundred recent tragedies just witnessed. "You have to evacuate," they said. I asked if this was it, if there was no way it could be stopped, if there was a five percent chance it wouldn't jump the road, take my house and roar unleashed into Los Padres Forest behind? "It's coming," they repeated. "It's our job to tell you that, help if needed." They didn't want my questions. They tolerated my foolish queries like impatient parents. I was asking the impossible, what everyone asked them, "Do you think there's a chance it might stop before reaching here?" "We'll take you out with us," they offered with no emotion, not wanting to waste one more precious moment on another fool who thought he might be the enchanted one, the one to escape the obvious fiery odds of fate. Watching them descend the driveway winding through the olive grove none of us contested their message of doom. Already the flames jumped another ridge, filling the entire cañada, an erratic four-mile fire front with only one way to go, up. Up over the mountain road, through the olive orchard, fueled by two hundred years of growth, up through the redwood trees, palm trees, orange trees, up to the Casa, whipping along the terrace of the veranda, catching the massive timbers, flaming trees falling onto the tile roof. That

was *it*. The one thing I forgot to do. We had to cut the tall olive trees that could fall on the house. My brother started the chainsaw. The sound of wind in our ears already louder than the cutting whine of the saw's engine as we sliced through tree trunks four times wider than our bodies. One seventy-foot tree cracked and split down the middle, high winds twisting it around as it fell crashing onto a corner of the house. We jumped from the erratic line of fall to avoid being crushed beneath a ton of hard timber.

The approaching fire's intense light was no brilliant night became day. We dumped all excess gasoline from the saw in the middle of the firebreak completed around the Casa that day. My wife set the terrified doves free. They scattered, soaring up and above the wall of flame which appeared to advance across the road into the olive grove. We retreated like a broken army to a slight knoll affording a view down into the Casa, passing by a neighbor's house. He stood on his balcony with a bottle of Wild Turkey whiskey in one hand, the full blast of Verdi's *Requiem* chorus thundering from speakers at the rolling flames. Only in Santa Barbara do people fight fires to classical music. Ascending the knoll we saw the fire had not yet jumped into the orchard. Below the Casa bulldozers attacked on all fronts, trying to break up the implacable wall of flame. None of us spoke of what seemed imminent: nothing could stop the fire now. The announcer on a blaring transistor radio excitedly reported the last houses on Mountain Drive were directly in the fire's path. That meant us. The knoll was a strategic position, from it we could determine if the fire would engulf the Casa or cut straight

up the steep arroyos to the sides, allowing us the chance to race down and make our stand at the most threatening point. Our water supply had been cut, but we still had shovels and blankets. The wall of flames crested above the road below, the reality of its menacing light reflected in all our faces. Looking down at the Casa I noticed the orchard surrounding it, and all the soft green planting I had done to make it a spiritual sanctuary, was no longer a bit of esthetic fancy, but a magnificent pile of manmade fuel.

The radio announcer shouted the last five houses on Mountain Drive finally burst into flames. It was strange, hearing someone declare one's house burning, when below the Casa still stood, its tile roof reflecting like a red flag before a charging bull. The announcer could barely contain the thrill in his voice, screaming there was no way the thousand firemen and more than one hundred pieces of heavy equipment could prevent the blaze from going into the National Forest. "Who knows," he panted, "maybe all of California is about to go up in smoke?"

With the dawn the wind stopped. The wall of flame dropped steadily like the phosphorescent ebbing of a moonlit tide. Not one of us could believe it. The Casa was going to survive. As the sun feebly poked through thick black clouds hanging over the ocean the scene of devastation spread out before us, a vast and enormous sweep of scorched earth, nearly the entire Cañada del Coyote reduced to ashes. On distant ridges of the Riviera was the rubble of hundreds of houses, some still flaming high, the ocean behind steelgray with low-lying layers of smoke. My brother broke the silence, saying softly he now knew what it

felt like to live through a bombing. We returned to the Casa,
thankful it was not a blackened pit, thankful not to spend the
day fending off scavengers and looters. But the day ahead
proved the longest of my life. The intensity of the holocaust left
behind hotspots of activity, capable of bursting any moment
into uncontrollable flame. Throughout the lower sections of the
cañada the fire was not "contained."

All day air tanker-bombers droned overhead, dropping tons
of fire-retardant chemicals on smoking brush and ashen pits of
former homes. Helicopters screamed on the far side of the
Riviera, dipping into the cement bowl of a reservoir like pre-
historic wingless monsters, scooping enormous dripping buckets of water, flying off with the swinging loads trailing from
umbilical cords of steel cable. The National Guard took control
of all roads leading into the cañada as firefighters from all the
Western states arrived to hack, saw and dynamite new fire
breaks up and down the ravines below us. Everyone dreaded
nightfall, for it threatened sundowner winds to fan the smol-
dering fire into sudden hideous life.

Through the long hot day we cut new fire breaks around the
property, felling more trees, pulling brush away from the Casa
into the middle of the garden, until fresh-cut branches and
limbs stood higher than six men. The radio was our only link
with the outside, informing the fire originated exactly where
the Great Coyote began thirteen years earlier. What started the
night before as the "Second Coyote Fire" now officially was
"The Sycamore Fire," named for the draw of land cutting
through the cañada between the mountains and the sea where a

hundred houses burned to the ground. The Sycamore was for-
tuitously triggered by a young man out for a kite-flying lark, the
string of the kite whipping out of control in strong sundowner
winds, wrapping around highvoltage wires juiced up by 1,600
volts of electricity. A splaying arc of sparks touched off the
holocaust.

Funny how life deals the deck. The twenty-year-old man who
"started the fire" was most certainly a sensitive soul, a life poet
and gentle being who would just as soon put an end to his own
life than set off a fury to ravage the lives of thousands. And in
the dry, blistering weeks preceding the fire there was another
man who sought a different sort of infamous glory, a man called
by Santa Barbara police the "Saturday Night Special." A man
who cruised the back mountain roads above town every Saturday night, flipping from his car window books of matches with
lit cigars secured to them by rubberbands. A sick soul lusting to
see beauty burn, who yearned for Coyote to howl and sirens
scream, a life-long loser who in the end couldn't even start a fire
by trying. Yet the kid with the kite was tapped on the shoulder
by fate. Funny how life deals the deck.

As sunset filled the cañada the scene was surreal and haunt-
ing. Air tankers and helicopters negotiated last flights over a
landscape of twisted and charred trees in dying light. It could
have been the scene of a beautiful desert sunset, except for
scores of naked stone chimneys poking like lonely fingers to
remind us where people lived only twenty-four hours before in
the heart of sub-tropical paradise. We waited for sundowner
winds to come up blowing like ancient furies. Below us ranks

of firemen swelled to nearly two thousand, brigades of bulldozers poised, the lines of battle drawn. The implicit tension in
the smoke-scented air was like that of war, the weariness of it
overtaking all of us waiting, watching. That night we slept
fitfully, small gusts of wind came up suddenly, and died as
suddenly.

Early in the morning I was awakened by a curious sound of
children laughing, but they were like wild children. I went to
the window. In dawn light I gazed into the garden where we
turned on sprinklers to wet down the whale-size pile of brush.
In the fine mist quick forms of coyotes astounded me. They had
come up from the burned-out cañada to the small oasis I had
created, chasing in circles on damp green grass, their laughing
call at once cheerful and playful. It was as if they had taken me
as their totem. Quickly as they appeared, they disappeared.
That morning all of my daughter's six white doves returned.

More than three days passed before I felt secure enough to
leave the Casa. Three days of living with fear the winds would
whip the remaining hotspots into another monstrous night-
mare of devastation. I drove along the twisting mountain road
to the top of Coyote Road. Carloads of tourists were nearly
bumper to bumper, pointing, ohhing and ahhing at a blasted
and blackened landscape where a thousand people once lived
and millions of dollars worth of damage occurred in nine hours.
Signs nailed to charred trees before ruined houses warned,
TRESPASSERS AND SIGHTSEERS WILL BE EATEN! At the
exact spot where the fire originated a family commanded the
middle of the road. The father held traffic back as his teenager

daughter spray-painted a giant white cross on black pavement. She stood up, her face radiant as she looked triumphantly at her father. Behind her were left the spray-painted words, TRUST IN JESUS, HE IS THE LAMB. I smiled and motioned her over. She hesitatingly took one step toward me but the father held her back, guarding her innocent air. "Trust in Coyote," I called. "What?" She ran a hand across the smooth, untroubled skin of her forehead as I drove away. I headed down the cañada where good friends lost everything. Potters, sculptors, writers, painters lost homes, studios, libraries, manuscripts, paintings, lifetimes of creations. I passed by what was the home of Christopher's Books publisher Melissa Mytinger, deep in the Sycamore Canyon at the bottom of Coyote Road. A place where the fire had been so intense its winds knocked people off their feet, firemen facing the fast wall of flames were trapped, covered themselves with aluminum-plastic "fire-shelters" and let the flames roar over. The heat so intense it melted Melissa's printing press down to a warped mass of pig iron. Everything was gone for Melissa, the press, the books, the private collection of memories. She single-mindedly sifted through ashes of her former life. Of all the fine books she printed, only one small page burned around the edges in a perfect oval was left, leaving a remarkable and stunning message from a book entitled *Coyote Tantras:*

Old Creator summoned them
to his tipi in center of clouds to help
him plan world. There were many arguments;
but they decided to make all rivers
flow in one direction; and that there should be
bends in the rivers so eddies would enable
fish to stop & rest.
They placed beasts in forests—human beings
would have to keep out of their way; humans
were not allowed to live forever.
All food would come from the soil
    Coyote wanted no responsibility
    "Guard the fire" he said
        & left.

Old Creator summoned
his tipi in center of clouds to help
him plan world. There were many arguments
but they decided to make all rivers flow
in one direction; and that there should be
bends in the rivers so eddies would enable
fish to stop & rest.
They placed beasts in forests—human beings
would have to keep out of their way; humans
were not allowed to live forever.
All food would come from the soil

Coyote wanted no responsibility
"Guard the fire" he said
& left

Acknowledgement is made to Melissa Mytinger and Barry Gifford
for permission to reprint lines from the book *Coyote Tantras*.

Cover design by Francine Rudesill
Designed and typeset in Garamond by Jim Cook
SANTA BARBARA, CALIFORNIA

LIBRARY OF CONGRESS CATALOGING-IN-PUBLICATION DATA
Sanchez, Thomas.
Angels burning.
(Capra back-to-back series; v. 10)
No collective t.p. Titles transcribed from individual title pages.
Texts bound together back to back and inverted.
1. Mountain life—California. 2. Coasts—California. 3. Wildfires—California.
4. Sanchez, Thomas. 5. Powell, Lawrence Clark, 1906- . 6. Malibu Region
(Calif.)—Biography. 7. Santa Barbara Region (Calif.)—Biography.
I. Powell, Lawrence Clark, 1906- . "Ocian in view." 1987.
II. Title. III. Title: "Ocian in view."
F866.S198 1987 979.4'91 87-10318
ISBN 0-88496-265-2 (pbk.)

PUBLISHED BY
CAPRA PRESS
Post Office Box 2068
Santa Barbara, California 93120

LAWRENCE CLARK POWELL

"Ocian in View"
The Malibu

Illustrated by Irene Robinson

VOLUME X

CAPRA PRESS
1987

THE CAPRA BACK-TO-BACK SERIES

VOLUME X
CAPRA BACK-TO-BACK SERIES

"Ocian In View"
THE MALIBU

Twenty years earlier and eighty miles south of the fire Sanchez describes is The Malibu, locale for Powell's essays when he too describes battling a wild fire through the night as it raced through arroyos, leaving only blackened ruin. He also writes of rain and flood, and of the natural life during those earlier Malibu years, the shore birds, denizens of tide pools and Chumash middens.

Powell was called "dean of western letters" by the *Los Angeles Times.* Librarians knew him as University Librarian and Dean of the Graduate Library School at UCLA, while readers know him as a longtime contributor to *Westways,* and author of a broad range of books, including *California Classics* and *The Blue Train.*

*The Back-to-Back Series provides a showcase
for shorter literary work from both established
and newer writers and is published by*

CAPRA PRESS
POST OFFICE BOX 2068, SANTA BARBARA, CALIFORNIA 93120

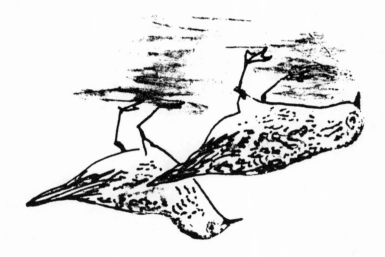

OCIAN IN VIEW

"OCIAN IN VIEW"

WILLIAM CLARK was a better explorer than speller. When he and Meriwether Lewis had made their way across the Missouri and down the Columbia and come at last in sight of what they had been so long in finding, Clark wrote in his journal, "Ocian in view. O, the joy!"

Ocean is in view as I write, our watery front-yard, disturbed by the westerly which has been blowing since yesterday, when it

9

swept away the overcast. Close in the water is sandy, then the
calm of the kelp bed, and beyond lies the dark sea with wind-
horses running wild on its surface. About a mile out, a tanker
from El Segundo is heading up coast, riding nearly awash, taking explosions of sea over the bows, sight of which recalls my
own life at sea, which began with a voyage round the world
when I was eighteen.

Mountains I love and desert and even a few cities, but I have
chosen to live what's left of my life here at continent's end, on
the hem of the sea, where the water nibbles away at property to
which we hold tenuous title.

Great poetry has been written about the sea, from Homer
through Shakespeare, to Melville and Matthew Arnold, Dana,
and Robinson Jeffers. Only geniuses and fools write poetry
about it, and I know I am not the one and hope I am not the
other. Keats had its discoverer staring at it silent in wild sur-
mise, but then Balboa (not Cortes) was exploring, not essaying.
And yet living beside it, seeing and hearing, smelling and feeling the Pacific Ocean, finds me moved to words, hopeful of
communicating the role of ocean in my life.

Buried first memories cannot be dredged up, even for the
sake of an essay. They go back to my infancy, for though born in
the District of Columbia, I came each year to California as a
baby, either to Riverside or Newport Beach; and when we
finally moved for good to South Pasadena, our summers were
spent on that spit of sand between sea and bay at Newport-
Balboa.

My father liked to fish, He also had means to buy softshell

crabs for bait. I dug and screened and imprisoned them live, then sold them to him for pocket money. He was a surf-fisher, while I preferred harpooning sharks in the shallow water over mudflats in the bay. I liked to go alone on the incoming tide clear to the backwaters known as The Lakes, deep in the Irvine Ranch, harpoon and fish there for hours, then row easily home on the outgoing tide. Later I went to sea with my father and Cap' Adams, in the latter's motorboat *Skipjack,* and we trolled for albacore in the Catalina Channel, and caught 'em too, big ones who preferred our jigs to being canned as Chicken of the Sea.

When I was fifteen my father died; we had less money then, and there were no more summers at the beach. Years later my girl and I used to go down to the sea again, on winter weekends, to a house on the bay front, built of sombre redwood, full of sweet smells and windy noises. There was no one on the beach, and all the wood and shells were ours to glean. It was before we were married, and the uncertain future met with loneliness of sea and sand to make it an experience we did not often repeat. We were not seasoned enough yet to be so much alone.

The round-the-world voyage came after my freshman year in college, and was taken for recuperation from a summer siege of 'flu. I went as a member of the ship's orchestra on the Dollar Liner, *President Harrison,* sailing from San Francisco November 10, 1925, on a cold gray afternoon when the swells began to lift the bow even before we had cleared the golden Gate. Liner? Passenger-carrying freighter.

During the four-month voyage we called at twenty-six ports,

including Hong Kong, Singapore, Port Said, Genoa, New York, Panama—places of squalor and beauty, of poverty and riches, all of which made lasting impressions on me, who had been an avid boy-reader of the little blue school geographies by Carpenter; and yet the most lasting of all impressions of that Magellanic voyage was that made by oceans and seas, seen at all hours, and different seasons, and in all weathers. I recall the rainswept run from Honolulu to Kobe, my first tropical sunsets between Manila and Singapore, the lonely waters of the Indian Ocean and the crowded Mediterranean, edged with colored stuccoes; and the North Atlantic in January during one of the worst storms ever measured, when the waves and the troughs between them were of vast dimensions, and the ship took a pounding. We were three days late on the run from Marseilles to Boston.

During the summer of 1928 I worked again as ship's musician, this time on the *Yale,* that slim white steamer with the thin black stacks which plied with her sister ship, the *Harvard,* between San Diego, San Pedro and San Francisco. We used to sail from the latter port twice a week at four o'clock, and by sundown were abeam the Santa Lucias, then picking up the lights of Sur and Piedras Blancas, as the darkness and the wind fell together.

The next long voyage came when I sailed for France on board the French Line freighter *Orégon,* San Pedro for Le Havre, calling at La Libertad and the ports at either end of the Panama Canal. It was the first time I had ever been a paid passenger on a ship, and I relished that twenty-eightday voyage, reading and

writing, eating well, learning French, sunbathing on the forward deck-cargo of squared fir logs or lying on the ledge at the apex of the bows, looking down at the cutwater and curl of ocean, as we drove through summer seas, scared once by sight of a shark as it followed the ship for hours, rolling over hungrily to show its teeth. Rainbow-colored jelly fish floated on the surface, and flying fish with iridescent wings sometimes flew on deck.

I came home from Europe in the *Majestic,* crossed the Atlantic again years later in the *Queen Elizabeth,* and returned in the freighter *American Scientist,* ever in love with ocean life, eager for the voyage to continue indefinitely, sensitive to changes of sea and sky, both subtle and sudden, delicate and brutal, addicted to the master smell of oil-hot machinery, and so conditioned by the pulse of the propeller shaft that when the engines were turned off, I felt that the ship had died, its heartbeat stopped.

Such are the memories that rise in me when, on mornings like this, I sit at cliff's edge and look down and out to sea.

The wind has risen even more to the degree described by mariners as "fresh," by no means a gale, but of such violence as to lift the kelp fronds, which usually lie on the surface, and fly them like amber banners. The seabirds have given up and gone to roost on the leeside of the rock cliffs; and if it were not for a pane of glass between me and the wind, I too would be driven into the roost we call house.

A great anthology could be compiled of sea poetry and prose, a job for my old age, when I hope I will be better read

than fifty finds me. If I had now to pick the one example which pleases me the most, it might well be the cry of William Clark—"Ocian in view. O, the joy!"

II

WE MOVED to the Malibu, twenty-eight miles up coast from campus, and my wife hasn't yet recovered from the shock. For years we lived close to the Library, and I was scornful of those who chose to inhabit such outlandish communities as West Covina, Compton, and Canoga Park, and had to spend hours each day in fighting traffic. Although she always wanted to live

at the beach, my wife had lost hope, for the nearby ocean
resorts were too built up to satisfy her desire for a large yard
and semi-wild garden, and she had come to take as gospel my
claim that I would never become a commuter. What happened?
It began with the stand of bamboo outside our bedroom window,
planted originally for the lullaby of its rustle. Then the
weather seemed to worsen (all changes in weather are blamed
on The Bomb, aren't they?) and the movement of evening air
slackened and finally ceased, and there was nothing but smog by
day and its stagnant aftermist by night, while the bamboo stood
somnolent. I longed for the mild aerial turbulence Southern
California once enjoyed.

There were other factors too in my change of feeling, such as
the growing up of our sons, which made it no longer necessary
that we live near schools, and my discovery that the Library got
along nicely without my presence every day, which had been my
bad habit during the years we lived near campus.

And so it came to pass that one day, in obedience to the inner
voice, I went home early and said to my wife, "We're going
househunting." She sat in amazed silence as I drove along San
Vicente Boulevard (reminiscent of the Santa Monica Road
Races of my boyhood), down canyon to the coast highway,
thence northwest beyond Topanga and Las Flores canyons,
Malibu Lagoon and the movie colony, the strand at the mouth
of Corral Canyon which some Floridan corrupted to Coral
Beach, then Látigo Canyon (accent on the primary, if you
please, it's Spanish for whip), past Paradise Cove and over the
neck of Point Dume (also a corruption, from Fray Dumetz, one

of the Franciscan missionaries in the eighteenth century), thence to the county beach at Zuma and adjoining Trancas and Encinal colonies, where the coast curves east and west—coast of the prevailing westerlies, testified to by windbreaks of blue-gums and cypress.

Only then did I slow up and sniff the air, pungent with kelp and conifers, mesembryanthemum and geranium, and we looked at one another.

"This will make the bamboo rustle," I said. "Now to find a place suited to our needs. I know it's here, but where?"

"You mean way out here?" my wife asked. "You'd be willing to live way out here?"

"It's still in the county, isn't it?" I countered.

She was speechless, and pleased.

The realtor had nothing for sale, but as we were leaving, his phone rang. Someone calling in to list a house. It sounded possible. The three of us went to investigate, and found it off the highway on the coast between Lechuza and Sequit points. We entered the yard through a grapestake fence, beneath untopped cypresses, and found ourselves straightway in a secret garden, planted to roses and lilies, dropping to terraces of gera-niums, hedged by pine, eucalyptus, and *Pittosporum crassifo-lium,* the silver-grey-leafed Australian which resembles the pineapple guava.

The garden grew to the brink of the palisade, bushed with wild bladder and buckwheat plants, and ankled a hundred feet below with sandy beach and blue water, and a few rocks to relieve the monotony. A cliff's edge cabana promised smoky

cooking. The sheltered patio was bright with bougainvillea, hibiscus, fuschias, camellias, and pacified by an olive tree.

It was a winter day, and we could see Santa Barbara Rock, forty miles due south, while the islands of Santa Catalina, Ana-

capa, and Santa Cruz lay closer on either hand. Behind us and to the west, the skyline of the chaparral-covered Santa Monicas was high and curving. Through a break in the trees, highway traffic could be seen but not heard.

I stole a look at my wife, and caught her stealing a look at me. She nodded. I nodded. The shock of recognition, and we had yet to enter the house. Surely not the way Benjamin Franklin would advise one to acquire property: to know you wanted it before you had even examined it. Or does he have a paragraph on instantaneous perception as a business asset?

Inspection proved the house fairly well suited to our needs and wants. If the kitchen was too small for her, so was the study too small for me; each sympathized with the other, thus maintaining the balance necessary for marital bliss. At least the garage had an ocean view window, which would please our car-loving

younger son, if during hours spent on visits home, he ever emerged from the bearing straits and looked out.

A series of obstacles, chiefly in selling our house in Palms, delayed the deal, but we never doubted, for we knew that house was meant for us; and thanks to patience and banker friends, the obstacles were overcome, and we moved to the Malibu.

"But isn't it windy?" our friends ask. "Don't you find the fog depressing? And what about that long drive into the sun, both morning and night?"

So I explained to these city-dwellers that windy air means fresh air, and how responsive we and the transplanted bamboo are to it. Our stretch of coast, more sheltered than Zuma and Dume, receives a brooming nearly every afternoon; and in the gray hours before the westerlies have swept the mist away, we hear the foghorns of the fishing boats, speaking of the need for cautious movement. Back in 1912 an Englishman named J. Smeaton Chase camped on the Malibu, while riding horseback from Mexico to Oregon, and wrote in the book he published afterward called *California Coast Trails,* "The breeze was strong and keen, and an inexhaustible freshness was in the air, as if the world had been created within the week." No change in the weather.

And the sixty-mile roundtrip? Not bad. The fast highway is a safe road if one keeps his eyes more on it than on the scenery. There are only a few signals between home and campus, and a neighbor tells us that if one finds favor in the Lord's eye, he can make all of them in green sequence. I'm working at it. The diesels that roll between Los Angeles and San Francisco run

interference for a Hillman, and when the setting sun dazzles, one can seek the shady slipstream of a Fruehauf and let the truck driver face the music.

Mornings I coast to work on the momentum of sound sleep and good breakfast, while the drive home in the evening brings me to the place a wag suggested we christen *El Sea Powell* more relaxed than my wife found me when we lived close to campus, the reason being that the forty-five minute drive home is just the time needed for the administrative sediment to settle.

III

AFTER WE moved to the Malibu my reading suffered a corresponding change, both sea and sierran. The coast beyond Point Dume is beautiful for its sandy beaches, kelp beds, crumbling palisades, and curving line of the Santa Monicas; so immediately beautiful that our television has been dark since we moved. All the hours are lovely in their lights and colors, wind

and calm; and if one isn't gardening or gleaning wood on the beach, swimming or walking, he is content to sit and watch the passage of time over the earth.

The only way to get any reading or writing done in this environment is to retreat to my study at the back of the house, pull the curtains to shut out sight of the mountains through the leaves of the olive tree, and sit facing the wall, yellow pad on my lap, blue pencil in my fist, and hope.

In moving to the new house my wife and I had twin hopes, she for a larger kitchen, I for a study that would once again shelve all of my books, as did my room in Beverly Glen and as the swallows'-nest study in the house on the Kelton hill did not. Neither was realized. Her ship's kitchen was even smaller, my study nearly the same size as Kelton, 9x12, a mere three-foot gain.

Though lacking a panoramic view, it has a bluegreen shed-roof ceiling, and golden pine walls which accommodate nearly fifty pictures and prints, including Tom Craig's water-color of the tawny hills back of Stanford, haired with oak, a mezzotint of Rembrandt's sombre portrait of his son Titus, and Conrad Buff's oil of Maynard Dixon's cool-house in Southern Utah, with its blue door, blue sky, and shimmering cottonwoods. An Oriental floor-rug, two prayer-rugs, and a pair of Asia Minor saddlebags, all from my father's collection. Two religious pictures in hand-carved olive-wood frames he brought from Florence half a century ago and which serve as a link between me and him, dead now nearly as long a time. A rose jar, put down in 1910, sweet as ever. Two abalone shells, heaped with smaller

shells sent by my brother Clark from the shores of the Indian Ocean. Book truck. Work table. Chair. Pallet for guest bed. Cherry-wood case for small books. Two oak-wood sections holding a thousand volumes. The Ellwood Queen, Joseph Muench's soaring photograph of the lemon-scented gum, eucalyptus *citriodora,* at Goleta. A Greek dancing maiden, equally queenly. The Dollar Line insignia from my musician's cap. Pig bank. Radio. Pictures of Fay, two of Mozart. Material possessions. Talismans. Warders off of evil. Things beloved, things fugitive. Mine for a time, then someone else's, then no one's; all doomed to "leave not a wrack behind."

There out of sight but not sound of the sea, breathing the ever present smell of ice plant, sea wrack, geranium, conifers, and bluegums, what have I been reading? Books about our new environment, the old Rancho Topanga Malibu Sequit. On the day of opening of the coast road back in 1928, after the long fight to gain a public right-of-way, I drove over it in a topless Hupmobile roadster from Santa Monica to Oxnard and back via Calabasas, an all-day trip, and even then the beaches were withheld by barbed-wire fence. I can still recall the sense of discovery I had during that first day on the Malibu, three hundred eighty-six years after Cabrillo.

Happy Days in Southern California by Frederick Hastings Rindge (1898) is a rare work by the former owner of the rancho, filled with details of shore and ranch life. Thus the owner had only himself to blame for having commenced the advertising which led people to come and squat on his land.

When I called for the book in the library's rare book room, I

was startled to see by the accession number—286063—that it was one of the first volumes I handled upon joining the UCLA staff in 1938, when I was given the task of accessioning the recently acquired Cowan collection. This copy was presented by the author to Robert Ernest Cowan.

Another example of a coming event casting its bibliographical shadow occurred in the second Malibu volume I read—*Sondelius Came to the Mountains,* by Madeleine Ruthven, a pamphlet of poems published in 1934 by the Primavera Press when I was one of its directors (assigned to the shipping room), along with Jake Zeitlin, Ward Ritchie, Phil Townsend Hanna, and Carey Mc-Williams. I had not re-read it since, and did not seem to own a copy. I found out why when I called for the UCLA copy: on August 11, 1938 it had been presented to the Library by L.C.P., and in the seventeen ensuing years it had stood unwanted in the stacks.

The poems are about the folklore and flora of the back country almost directly in from where we now live: Big Sycamore Canyon, Boney Ridge, Triunfo Pass, and the Yerba Buena road. Along with Hildegarde Flanner, W.W. Robinson, and C.F.

MacIntyre, Madeleine Ruthven is one of the few poets who has looked at the mountains of Southern California with eyes both sharp and loving.

During vacation we varied days on the beach with explorations of the back country Miss Ruthven wrote about, and were pleased to locate many of the landmarks just as she described them. The great stone house, whose creation she tells so beautifully, still stands on the sage-covered hill facing the battlements of Boney Ridge.

This end of the Santa Monicas, from Malibu Canyon west to Big Sycamore Canyon, a distance of perhaps twenty miles, and of a depth of ten or twelve from ocean to Ventura Boulevard, is lonely country. Too unspectacular to draw tourists, too dry to support many settlers, it slumbers undisturbed with few to breathe the incense of chaparral, or to see the gray fox cross the road, the hovering hawk, and the rare hunter without firearms, taking advantage of a special deer season in the Santa Monicas limited to the bow and arrow.

At the foot of Boney Ridge, approaching Triunfo Pass, the road traverses a many-acred stand of the brush known as red shanks, which was in full feathery bloom in August. To learn more about this member of the chaparral family I re-read one of the best of all botanical works of California, *The Elfin Forest of California* by Francis M. Fultz (Los Angeles, Times-Mirror Press, 1923), a small book with more than one hundred photographic illustrations by the author, which is about nothing but chaparral and the small pines of the Southern California mountains.

Botanically accurate and charmingly written, this book by a
retired educator and forester who lived in Highland Park
deserves reprinting. His death a few years ago brought Fultz's
papers to the UCLA Library, through the generosity of the
author's widow and the good offices of Glen Dawson. Let me
quote what he says about the virgin stand of red shanks we
came upon in our wanderings:

> A sister of the Chamise flourishes in the southern part of the
> Elfin Forest. It is *Adenostoma sparsifolium,* the specific
> name indicating one of its distinctive characteristics—thinly
> leafed. It is often called 'redshanks,' from the color of its
> trunk. It keeps shedding its bark in long, thin shreds, which
> gives it a rather untidy appearance. But this characteristic
> serves as an unfailing mark of identification. It is a much
> more robust shrub than its sister, the grease-wood, growing
> to double the diameter and nearly twice the height. It is
> plentiful about the western slope of Mt. San Jacinto, and
> from there southward. The only place that I have seen it
> north and west of the San Gabriel Valley is in the Santa
> Monica Mountains, where there is a patch of unusually fine
> specimens near Saddle Peak.

In his *Southern Sierras of California* (1924) Charles Francis
Saunders has a chapter on the Santa Monicas which includes
several delightful pages on the flowers of Malibu Creek, whose
gorge is now traversed by a road cut in the rock-face by convict
labor.

Dana was also on my summer re-reading list, and I savored
once again his *Two Years Before the Mast,* the first and best of

all books of marine Californiana. His descriptions of the coast from San Diego to Monterey are timeless. Holder's *Channel Islands of California* was consulted to see if it gives the flashing intervals of the Anacapa Light (it doesn't), and finally I returned to Chase's *California Coast Trails* to savor again what he said about the Malibu:

> Turning, then, westward, a few miles of pleasant road brought us to the entrance to the Malibu Ranch, a long strip of land lying between the southward-facing foothills of the Santa Monica Mountains and the shore. At the gate was posted a warning that Trespassing was Strictly Prohibited. I knew that public right of way through the ranch had long been contested by the owners, and I had been warned that I might find my way disputed by their myrmidons with shot-guns. But there was nothing except the passive placard to prevent my entering, and I passed on with little doubt of making an equally peaceful exit at the western end."

Chase camped that night by the lagoon at Trancas Canyon, and to this day one of the Ridge's range-rider's shacks stands nearby, boarded up and ruinous. The following night he slept on the beach farther upcoast. "I was up at four o'clock, and broke camp early. The breeze was strong and keen, and an inexhaustible freshness was in the air, as if the world had been created within the week. After a few miles more of alternate shore and cliff, we crossed the line into Ventura County, and at the same time bade adieu to the Malibu and its cantankerous but futile placards."

IV

MY BOYHOOD and youth were nourished by the San Gabriels
and the San Bernardinos which together form the Sierra Madre
range of Southern California. It was not until I went to work at
UCLA, twenty years ago, and moved near to the campus that
allegiance was transferred to the Santa Monicas, a less spectacu-

lar range which rises in Hollywood and extends fifty miles northwest to a marine ending at Point Mugu.

From living in Beverly Glen, I came to love the surrounding range of chaparral, oak, and sycamore. It was a good place for our sons to live as little boys, and now that they are grown to manhood, they find their subconscious minds full of memories of their mountain boyhood.

Although as I have already written, I discovered the western-most part of the range in the poems of Madeleine Ruthven, it was not until a decade later in 1944 that I came actually to know this remote area. At war's end my friend Gordon Newell, the sculptor, and his wife Emelia acquired land on the north slope of the mountains, overlooking Seminole Hot Springs, and it served me as a kind of retreat from too much city. From driving and walking and talking to Newell, I came to know and to love his land and the sea of chaparral which enislanded it. The north slope of the Santa Monicas is green the year round from springs, one of which he had deepened and rock lined, so that it was an unfailing source of cold water, even in the dryest summer. Through the years I watched him quarry honey-colored flagstone, sift and sack oak leaf-mould, breed Nubian goats, keep bees, carve wood and cut stone, while his wife made delicate jewelry and airy mobiles, and their children grew and grew—in some ways a twentieth-century Theocritean idyll.

It takes time to assimilate the essences of a land. When after years of residence in Inyo County Mary Austin wrote *The Land of Little Rain,* her publishers wanted her to move around the country, writing similar books about the other places of resi-

dence. Her reply was that it would take her ten years in a locale to be able to evoke its spirit, as indeed she did later for Arizona-New Mexico in *The Land of Journeys' Ending*.

Thus although we moved to the Malibu, in the seaward lea of the Santa Monicas, as recently as 1955, I brought to the land years of slow growing knowledge and deepening love for this country "where the mountains meet the sea"; and I was ready to write about it, not as a stranger. In fact it was this long background of reading and seeing that motivated our move—that and the feeling we have always had for the seashore. Plus something else, instinctive, mysterious and right.

So it was a kind of magnetic homecoming, our move to the Malibu, and now our leisure time is divided between shoreline walks and mountain drives.

On that coast the seasons merge almost imperceptibly into each other. When the rainy season is regular, then it is easier to know the time of year. When drought comes, how is one to know summer and fall from winter and spring? by the stars to be sure, and the position of the sun—those heavenly clockworks that transcend earthly times of wet and dry.

In the late autumn the evening wears Vega like a blue white diamond. Arcturus has set long before the sun did. Capella comes up over the mountains, brightest of the northernmost stars, and toward midnight, when Sirius is well risen, there directly below it, just above the horizon, appears the sky's number two glitterer, the southern star Canopus, never rising high enough to get beyond the city's atmosphere, which lends it a baleful light.

The sun which in summer set behind the mountain has moved out to sea, dropping from sight at the point where San Nicolas Island lies, if we were high enough to see it. See it we did from the crest of the mountains, on one of the day's end drives which conclude our otherwise stay-at-home Sundays, lying between Santa Barbara Rock and the Santa Cruz-Anacapa conjunction, eighty miles out, dark whale on the blue sea, never to be seen from shoreline.

Living on the Malibu one can choose between many peaceful things to do—stay at home and read or write or garden and other chores, or just sit; or drive in the hills; or walk on the beach. There is choice too among the hill drives—whether it be up the Decker Road along Mulholland, and down the Arroyo Sequit to the sea again, or up Little Sycamore Canyon on the Yerba Buena Road, over Triunfo Pass with a view to Lake Sherwood, then down past the lake, through Hidden Valley, over the hills and down Long Grade Canyon to Camarillo and the coast highway; or west from Little Sycamore along narrow roads leading into cul-de-sacs, where one sees foxes and hawks, and water flowing out of rockɛface—all of

this within fifty miles of Los Angeles, unknown to the millions.

Last autumn, when the first of the two recent fires swept over the mountains from the valley, leaped the crest of Boney Ridge and devoured the forest of red shanks which graced that mountain's southern slope, we feared a long bareness for the burned flanks. Winter rains brought a myriad of flowers in places where the sun had not penetrated for years, and then in the spring we rejoiced to see rise from the base of the burned chaparral delicate new growth. The fire had not proved mortal, though ten years would be needed for the forest to recover.

Summer's flowers succeeded spring's pinks and blues and whites—orange monkey-flower, red gooseberry, and the purple sage, bee heaven on earth—while the arroyos became seco and sand choked the creek-mouths.

By summer the winter's creekwood had all been gathered, and the gleaning was again of plankwood cast up by the sea, that and shells and fragments to serve as gravel on the garden paths. All these years I had remembered the crushed abalone shells with which Una and Robin Jeffers gravelled their paths at Tor House, and now I began to strew our walks with shells and bones and jeweled bits from the seashore.

The Chumash who dwelled here were jewelry makers, and the Southwest Museum preserves examples of their necklaces of tideline treasures. Now I see why. The wash of water renders all things smooth, and after high tide recedes, one finds the beach strewn with beautiful fragments. Westward I walk, stooping, picking, filling the cloth bag I carry, until it becomes leaden

and the way back weary. And when at last I empty it out on the path at home, the scattering iridescences and pearly bits—blue-black of mussel, flesh-pink of cowrie, purple of abalone—make a display Tiffany's should envy, and I am moved to acquire a polishing wheel, a cutter and a borer, a ball of cord, and become a necklace-maker. The abalone shells of this coast were prized by the Hopis far to the east, who ground them for dye tincture. These mollusca are rarely exposed by even the lowest tide, seeking the safety of deeper water, and even then skin-divers need powerful leverage to pry them loose, and woe to the man whose hand is caught. Freshly caught and sauteed in butter they are delicious, and their shells remain, forever beautiful.

Indians are buried everywhere from Mugu Lagoon to Malibu Creek. Every bulldozing operation brings their bones and artifacts to light, as one did just across Broad Beach Road from us—a dozen huddled skeletons, four or five hundred years old, taking no notice of their noisy resurrection. Our geranium garden, falling to Encinal Creek, is sure to be a burying ground, the diggers tell us. Mary Austin writes of the residue of personality that always haunts a place once inhabited by man. Jeffers' poetry is full of these hauntings. But I cannot say that I have encountered spirits here on the Malibu. Perhaps the diesels drive them away. I have no fear of them however. The Chumash were a gentle people, living on shell fish, roots, and acorn meal. We who are carnivorous may leave a different residue. Sometimes I wonder who will follow us here, and what they will make of our artifacts—books and discs and Scriptos, and less tangible, though perhaps more lasting, our love for this marine mountainscape called the Malibu.

V

ALONG THE MALIBU there has been a good aftermath of the storm, and the coast has been gathering manna. Mushrooms and other edible fungi rose overnight, and lived briefly in the light of day before consummating a buttery union in the skillet. Mustard greens likewise had a short life-span before they too yielded up on the stove. Last year's stalks were rooted out by the

34

wind and piled like skeletons against the fences, to make room for the new growth now in its head-high yellow prime.

Mussels also are in season—no delicacy, true, but few meals are more satisfying than a mess of them, gathered at ebb tide in the twilight, then steamed open and dunked in lemon-butter, salty, sandy, tough little guys, tasting of kelpy iodine, an atavistic feast linking us with our predecessors on this coastal shelf, who gave names to many of the places, from Anacapa and Hueneme to Mugu, Malibu, and Topanga.

Now we know why they inhabited the lagoons at the creek-mouths, for when the rainy runoff swells these arroyo secos to savage streams, the rivers break their summer sandbars and run to the sea, bearing treasure to the tidelanders. We live on the cliff by the estuary of Encinal Creek, and at the height of the storm when we went down with shovels to divert raven-ous runoffs, we saw the little watercourse, long barred from union with the ocean and held in stagnant continence, changed to a torrent, and raging out of the Santa Monicas to an eager consummation with the sea.

The Pacific was belying its name, roiled up for a mile off shore, wind-blown, coffee-colored, perilous to all but its native denizens—and I doubt they were pleased with the turmoil. We dwell on an open coast, with few shelters for small craft, and the shoreline is that seen by Cabrillo, Drake, Vancouver, and Dana, and in our day by the crews of purse-seiner, tuna-clipper, and tanker. The Catalina and Santa Barbara channel affords scant protection from southwesterlies, and the islands themselves are mostly steep and forbidding on both their lee and windward sides.

Life on the Malibu is richest at the creek-mouths, the Chumash knew; and so did we, after the storm was over and the runoff from the mountains washed upon the beaches. What a haul of firewood for the gleaning! We envy the Brents, whose open fireplace will take logs up to ten feet in length. Ours is only twenty inches wide, which means that sawing, chopping and splitting must follow gleaning and hauling.

It is years since the hills received such a scouring, yielding logs and stumps, burned roots, and rotting branches of oak, sycamore, red shanks and chamisal, much of it smashed to

fireplace length in its fall down the streambeds, and sculptured into beautiful shapes.

The sea itself casts up wood, smoothed by wind and wave— empty packing-cases of water-chestnuts from Hong Kong and ammunition boxes from Navy vessels, flawed planks of pine, Douglas fir, oak and redwood, cast overboard from lumber schooners, flotsam, corks from fisherman's nets, an occasional Japanese glass float, battered lobster traps, and sundry jetsam not worth its salt.

The first step is to cache the wet wood and let it dry, before carrying it up the path to the cliff-top. If one posts his pile with a sign reading "Blest be he who leaves my logs; Curst be he who steals my sticks," he is certain to find it when he returns, and just half its weight.

The joy of gathering beachwood is matched by that of burn-ing it, although an occasional twinge is felt, like eating one's pet rabbit, when a shaft of skin smooth chaparral is reduced to silvery ash. This wild wood's smoke has its own smells, differ-ent from those of domestic firewood—oak and walnut per-fumey, eucalyptus acrid, orange bittersweet, and juniper like incense—and unless it has been submerged a long while, it does not burn with a blue flame. One twelve-foot length of 2x4 was difficult to identify. From its weight and grain and color I called it oak. When I began to saw it, I realized my error. The fra-grance was like the interior of our clothes closet. Cedar! The smoke from its burning was even sweeter.

Characteristic of this coast is the offshore wind that blows after dark, very faintly, a mere breath of mountain air suspiring

delicately toward the sea, bearing smells of sunwarmed brush and stream-bed with smoke from our chimney, ghosts of the beach-wood, drifting down over the dark sand and water, residue of fire, liberated energy, sweeter far than incense of cathedral.

Now winter's constellations are risen high, Sirius ruling the zenith and fiery Canopus, describing his short arc above the southern horizon. In the west the lighthouse opens like an eye, then closes, leaving the night darker than before. In the east, when it is very clear, the Point Vicente light can be seen on the Palos Verdes, and nearer, the light buoy off Point Dume. These smells and sights assure one that he can leave the world to the wakeful and seek his bed, with the final thought that another storm will find us in the wood business.

VI

Life on the Malibu is not without its hazards. Rainstorm is one. When ten inches fell in thirty-six hours, the cliffs grew sodden and began to slide, and we learned the uses of sandbags. Then fire. As one who grew up in Southern California, I thought I knew all there was to know about forest and brush fires. From our house in Pasadena I had watched the wide face

of the mountains burn. Later I fought fire in the San Bernardinos near Forest Home. In La Crescenta during the autumn of
1933, we saved Poet MacIntyre's cabin from the flames, only to
loose it to flood on New Year's Day. For six years we lived in
Beverly Glen, a canyon in the easternmost Santa Monicas, and
there taught the boys the peril of open fires and wind, and were
relieved when we quit the canyon for the open plain.

On the ocean edge of the westernmost Santa Monicas, we
seemed to be protected from fire by three roads and fields
which separated us from the mountain, and also by the prevailing westerlies which would drive fire back over the mountain
away from the shore.

It was wind that nearly brought our ruin—not westerly wind
though, but the hated north wind, whose name in Southern
California is the Santa Ana. All fall it blew, often for days at a
stretch, bringing the brush to explosive dryness. No rain had
fallen since spring.

Christmas Day was dry and clear, and from indoors the sea
was beautiful, driven offshore by the wind which came in gusts
from the north, so that one could see the wind devils whirling
over the water in clouds of spindrift, finally disappearing out to
sea.

While waiting for the lamb to roast, I ventured a shell-gath-
ering walk at low tide. My naked body felt the blown sand like a
whip, and at the fiercest, I had to brace myself to keep from
being blown away. Gulls were soaring and swooping, and cormorants rode the wind like jets, headed eastward to their feeding beds. A couple of the curlew-like birds known as marbled

godwits took off ahead of me with foolish cries, their outspread wings changing their drab appearance while feeding to the black and white splendor which gives them their name. I took shelter behind a rock, directly beneath the ruin halfway up the cliff of one of the "depots" on the Queen's railway. Still to be seen also were a couple of rails and redwood ties.

The wind was still savage when we went to bed at ten, the sky swept clear, aglitter with stars, Anacapa flashed itswarning light. The cypresses, pines, and eucalyptuses were noisier than the surf. Cats' fur threw sparks when stroked. We slept in spite of the sinister atmosphere.

I woke abruptly at four to see a fierce glow in the sky. I arose instantly, knowing what it meant. Fire. From the bedroom's west window, the point of origin seemed north. I went to my study and looked out the window through tossing foliage. What I saw made me shout, and brought my wife on the run. Fire? God, the whole face of the mountain was burning, in a long line just below the summit, and moving toward us on the wind. Fear dried my mouth. I knew doom when I saw it.

Swiftly I dressed in shirt, pants, and shoes, while my wife, equally silent, corralled the four cats and one dog in our bedroom and shut the door.

In the patio we could smell the smoke and feel the heat. While I began to couple our garden hoses and prepare to wet down the cypress, potential torches, and the garage section of our roof not covered by tiles, my wife called the County Fire Station at Zuma to ask if a general alarm had been sounded. "At 2:30," the operator said. "Haven't you been alerted to evacuate?" No.

Our neighborhood and the highway were silent. Of the ten houses in our colony, only three were inhabited. The others had gone away for Christmas. Next to us new occupants, the man convalescing from an operation, took our advice and left by the highway west to Oxnard. It was still dark.

Then we phoned James Hartzell, a neighbor who was at his other home in Beverly Glen, thirty miles away. Half an hour later he had arrived and joined us on the hose line. Fell in back of a sheriff's car, he said, and made a fast run. Eventually we owed more to him, and the Killinger brothers, than to anyone else.

Sparks came like bullets on the wind, as the fire neared the highway. Occupants of two houses at the very foot of the mountain were setting backfires, their horse and burro beginning to whinny and bray in terror.

We made our decision not to load our animals in the car and leave, as others were doing, but instead I drove the station wagon down the road to the foot of the cliff in front of us, and we prepared to carry the cats down and lock them in it. Pippin, the big orange male, was too wild to hold, and ran off and hid. While carrying the two young males, Junior and Joey, down the path through the geraniums, my wife turned her ankle and dropped the cats and they too hid. So we ended, I carrying Besa, the toy poodle, and she carrying Mei ling, our old Siamese. Back up at the house we found it enveloped in smoke and sparks, and once again we were driven to the beach below, abandoning everything except my wife's handbag and my briefcase.

From the beach we saw fire on both sides and in back of our

house. A neighbor's wife joined us, carrying a bottle of water, a jug of brandy, and a revolver, and leading the horse and Sugar, the burro, from higher up. These latter I took charge of, and tied them to a post at the foot of the cliff, both docile as long as they were not separated.

My wife reconnoitered along the beach and returned to report a holocaust to the east of us. To the west the fire had come down Encinal Canyon and the neighbor was certain her house was burning, in spite of the valiant fight being waged by her husband to save it. Ours seemed doomed. We were somehow calm and resigned, having passed the point of concern for material possessions. Of a thousand beloved books, save which few? Pictures, records, clothes, the Steinway? Absurd. The mind, detached, said Let them burn. But the eyes turned away, unwilling to watch.

Still I ventured a look at our house on the cliff, little low whiteboard-sided dwelling, with slanting red-tile roofs, clinging to the earth in the dark grove of trees, and I saw it was not yet burning. The wind had veered due west. So I wrapped a wet towel around my face and went up, and just in time. The cabana was beginning to catch fire from a burning mattress laid alongside it for sunbathing. I dragged the mattress to the middle of the lawn, just as Pippin made a flying leap and landed on my shoulder, his favorite riding-place. So I took him down and shut him with Mei ling and Besa in the station wagon. Later Joey and Junior came safely out of hiding.

Then we went back up to the house and joined Hartzell in fighting the fire, which had reached our very road, and was

burning fences, cypresses at their base, weedy lots—everything
but the houses themselves. We used dribbling hoses—water
was giving out—shovel, hoe, wet sacks, anything, for we knew
that if one house caught fire, all would be lost. The Brents and
the Clarkes came from up coast and helped. We lost track of
time. The sun rose, blood red through smoke. Presently my
wife came hobbling among us with a tray of lamb sandwiches
and milk, a goddess of plenty, no less.

When we had control of these small fires, Hartzell and I
moved along the front and found the four Killingers, down
from their homes high on the Decker road, fighting to save the
houses toward which the fire in the cliff brush was being driven
by the changed. wind. They seemed to be up to their waists in
flame. This was what my wife had seen burning and thought all
the houses were afire, so thick was the smoke from flaming
cypresses. By some miracle our trees had not caught fire, perhaps because the wind was so fierce, though they were scorched.

Get a pumper engine! they cried, and I ran back to the west,
where Hartzell reported a county engine had arrived and was
trying to save the two houses at the mouth of Encinal Creek.
They had been successful. Only trees and outbuildings were
burning. One was the old range rider's shack.

The engine captain, come all the way from Downey in the
eastern part of the county, would not heed my plea, having been
ordered to stay put until danger was passed. But he used his
radio to ask for another engine to be sent to the other danger
point. Ray Rowe and his wife were fighting to save their house,
and lost only an outbuilding, thanks to the help of a pumper.

So back I ran, to find the Killingers and Hartzell, all but afire themselves, joined by two Edison Company linemen bearing a chemical tank with which they laid down a fireproof line on the bush. Down on the beach I saw a blundering possum. Most of the wild life had fled in the other direction.

It was then eight o'clock in the morning, and the worst was over on our stretch of Broad Beach Road. All day, though, we fought flare-ups, and by mid-afternoon Hartzell and I were down in Encinal Creek, seeking to quench a stubborn fire in the mesembryanthemum that had just reached and ignited a neighbor's board fence, leading like a fuse to a grove of cypress against the house itself.

From its thick green look, one would think that ice plant would not burn. Wrong. Under the green fleshiness are the old dry stalks through which fire spreads, slowly dehydrating the green growth above, until finally all is consumed.

We had commandeered all the garden hoses in the colony, and coupled them in two long lines, each of which dribbled water, but enough.

A couple driven out of Encinal Canyon by the advancing fire, came by in their pick-up truck, and showed us what they had chosen to save: their dog and parrot, the man's stamp collection, an extra pair of shoes for him (both lefts, one brown, one black), and his wife's cleaning rags (mistaken for her drawer of silk underwear). Later they returned and found their house had been saved by a heroic pumper unit from Zuma Fire Station, specially dispatched by the captain for whom the man had once done a carpentry favor. Bread cast upon the waters . . .

Our telephone was dead, so we drove to Zuma Lifeguard Station and got through to my secretary to spread the word to family and friends that we were safe. Our sons never did succeed in getting through the road blocks until the fire was out.

Late afternoon we drove west to the Brent's and found the fire coming down the mountain to the highway and the houses beyond, just as it had to us twelve hours earlier. There had been ample warning, however, and animals had been evacuated, including thirty-eight dogs from a kennel, and many Ventura County pumping units were present. No houses west of us were lost, save back in the canyons—Sequit and Little Sycamore— which were burned out, all but the winter-bare sycamores along the stream-bed. Those lovely arroyos lay in blackened ruin; the birds and small animal dead or homeless.

There was nothing we could do to help, and we barely regained our neighborhood, before the fire reached the road and swept across it to the very sand and sea.

Still the wind blew, savage and unrelenting, hour after hour. Our hair was grey with ashes, our eyes red from smoke. There was no water for several hours. The sour smell of burned brush was everywhere. All evening I patrolled the cliff and the cypress wind-breaks with hoe and shovel, seeking to keep the wind from scattering the embers of chaparral roots and redwood fence-posts. Hartzell returned to Beverly Glen at sundown, with my assurance that I could control the situation.

Milk and coffee were our only food, as between patrols my wife and I sat at the west window and watched the fire burn away from us along the coast—a fireworks display such as we never wish to see again. It was also going northward over the mountain, and we had a guilty feeling of security in knowing that, except for our immediate trees, there was nothing left to burn for miles around.

Throughout the night I kept on the alert, making half-hour sorties around the deserted neighborhood, shovel on my shoulder. Down in Encinal Creek oak and sycamore trunks were still burning. We were alone, except for an occasional State Highway Patrol car, on guard against looters. Eight houses on the beach were burned; scores more, on toward Point Dume.

Sometime after midnight I had a bad fright when I saw a glow in the cypress trees and thought they were afire. It was the rising moon seen through smoke. My mouth had gone dry again with a recurrence of the morning's symptom.

After twenty-one hours on her feet my wife went to bed and slept, the animals gathered around her—a most beautiful still-life. I blew out the candle she had lit, unable to bear any sight of fire, and tiptoed away. The wind would not let me even doze. Cold milk was my sustenance.

At four o'clock the wind finally dropped, twenty-four hours after we had awakened. I lay down in my dirty clothes on the sofa in the living room and slept for two hours.

Coffee at six was the best drink of my life. I felt equal to the day's work. It was another day before my body began to ache. By noon the deputy sheriffs had arrived, and our roads were sealed off by round-the-clock sentries from the curious and the would-be-looters. I would have had no compunction in shooting any trespasser, so savage were my feelings from the horror of destruction. Rats from the hills were beginning to overrun the coast. Our cats now earned their keep, while Besa served as a pointer.

Later I drove down coast to Zuma Fire Station, headquarters for the fighters and their machines, which had arrived from as far away as San Diego and San Luis Obispo, and found it like a scene behind battle-lines—hundreds of men, arriving and leaving, eating and resting, with heavy equipment of all kinds, some pieces with engines idling, the air full of a rumbling at once fearful and reassuring. The county services had performed heroically.

This was fire on the Malibu in Christmas week of 1956. A

hundred dwellings were burned. There was no consolation in the words of the County Fire Chief who said, "There is only one thing certain. It will happen again."

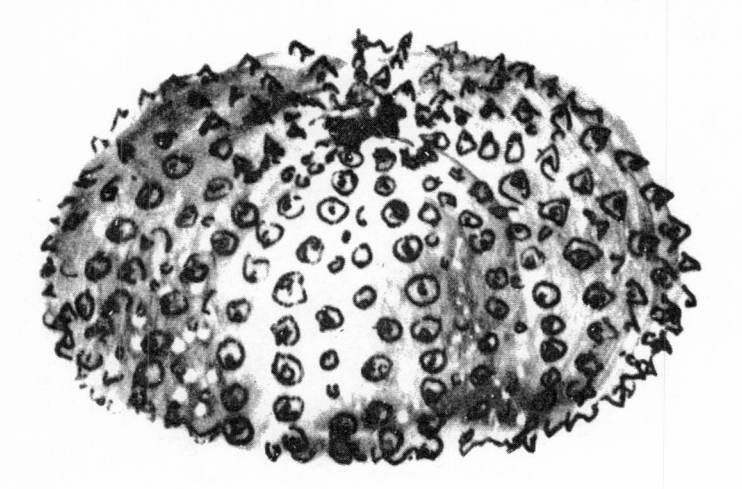

VII

AFTER FLOOD and fire things are peaceful again, hills greening after rain, the round of hours beautiful with the harmony of life. This is what all men seek and few men find. Now I know what Jeffers meant in speaking of his life at Carmel, before the death of Una, when he said, "I should be glad to live like this for several centuries; but good and evil are very cunningly balanced

in the most favored lives, and I should not consider myself ill-used if I were to die tomorrow, though it would be very annoying."

In order to maintain this balance in my own life and to propitiate evil, I have devised rituals of prayer and offerings, aimed at keeping myself thankfully in a state of grace for the blessings the Malibu has brought—a primitive practice which should not offend the ghosts of the aborigines. Looking back on it now, our escape from the Fire was miraculous. Or was it because we had passed the point of concern for material possessions, that the Lord allowed us to keep our home?

What next? Cliff slippage? Earthquake? Drought? Plague? War? All have visited the earth at some time in history. Southern Californians should not expect immunity forever.

Returning to Jeffers, he once explained his poetry as a means of warding off evil by creating poetical characters who would divert bad spirits from his household. Now I understand his intention. My prayers are said out of doors, uninsulated by wood and tile; my litanies are launched on the night wind before I go to bed. The outer magnificence here makes ridiculous indoor worship.

In New Mexico and Arizona *sky determines;* on the Malibu *ocean determines.* When city people ask silly questions, I realize that although they live in Los Angeles, ostensibly a seaport, they have no relationship with the ocean, other than to dip in it when the radio tells them the temperatures of sea and sky are safe for their health. Between Santa Monica and Big Sycamore, a distance of thirty-five miles, there are often several variations

of weather in the course of the hour's drive. I could not say which I like the most, a day of sun, when the heat radiates from even the water, or one of blown sand and spindrift, or the smother of windless fog, or mist, or driving rain. My wife feels differently. Gray weather depresses her, because she is a practical woman and wants sun for growing flowers and drying clothes.

I rise in the darkness before dawn, build up the fire from the night's coals, turn cats out, leaving dog to sleep,and sniff the air for the day's smells. Visitors have remarked that our colony smells like Carmel. That would be because of sunwarmed or fogwet cypress, pine, and geranium.

Then I make coffee, sit in front of the fire, and consider the state of the world. If it seems able to revolve without my help, I begin to write—correspondence, reports, reviews, or a talk, and continue until the light shows in the east. If it is a clear day, then sunrise over Point Dume is beautiful, Catalina dark against the sky. The newspaper hits the gate around seven. I take it with coffee to my wife in bed, then I breakfast on milk and fruit, and begin to think about the change to city man.

Since living on the Malibu, I go to work earlier and leave for home sooner than before. Unless there are evening demands, I try to leave campus by four-thirty, and when I turn off San Vicente Boulevard and corkscrew down Santa Monica Canyon into 101 A, see the ocean on my left, never the same shade of blue or green, peacock, salty, milky, turquoise, opalescent, amethystine, halcyon or wind-capped, and the curve of the mountains around the bay to Point Dume, then I love the route, every

mile of it, in both directions, at any time of day, the ribbon of road between sea and sierra, past Topanga and Las Flores, the Colony, Malibu Lagoon, and the canyons and coves clear to the Point, and then up and over its neck and the fall to Zuma Beach—another world, a better world.

In winter I reach home at sunset, shed suit for wool shirt, slacks and sandals, then have a drink with my wife, and watch the sea and sky change and darken, as the animals come in for the night. When the days lengthen, there is time for a walk on the beach before dinner, or a swim. Lacking a dining room, we eat at a candlelit table by the sea window, or by the fire. The cormorants go by on their westerly way, moving as fast as head wind allows, urgently bound for their island roosts. In contrast, the gulls float gracefully to their nearby cliff dwellings, while down on the beach tiny sandpipers tarry till dark, rolling in and out as though on invisible wheels, with the come and go of the water, dining on Crustacea. Or pelicans, dropping like doom on their dinner.

Our animals come close, but don't beg. They get handouts when they are good. There is Princess Mei ling, our little Siamese, born in April 1943, and still as temperamental as ever. The Orange Pippin, with his fondness for riding on my shoulder, and scuffling with our younger son when he is home overnight. The two toms, Joey and Junicr, which my wife found as abandoned kittens on the beach. They look upon Besa as their mother, and she rules them with loving authority. She is a good watchdog too. Sometimes in the still of a moony night, when sea lions surface and bark, Besa explodes like a pack of firecrackers.

Sundays are the best days, and the round of hours revolves from dark to dark with beautiful things between. Then I often write till mid-morning. If it is the page for *Westways,* I work in my study where the books are piled, and where the store of memorabilia—books, pictures, relics from different periods of my life, all of which I once consigned to the flames—makes good medicine and the words stream from the Scripto.

The rest of Sunday is for pruning, weeding, sweeping, and raking, or chopping and sawing. Our land is an acre, all planted, and we are the only gardeners. Roses bloom the year round, the eucalyptus seems to flower whenever it feels like it, the geraniums are dormant in summer, then explode into bloom when it rains. Springtime brings sweet alyssum, breaking over the yard in waves of fragrance. Camellias—the beauty called Colonel Fiery. Bougainvilleas. Copa de oro. Purple and yellow lotus blooms of the mesembryanthemum. Along the cliff the

coreopsis gigantea, most of the year a dead stalk, feathers out green and bears the golden flower that gives it name.

Each spring the same mockingbird has returned to entertain us with his repertoire of imitations: crow, quail, meadowlark, duck, frog, dog, cat. We are waiting confidently for him to mock the "song" of Sugar, the burro. In summertime the migrating monarch butterflies drift by in orange-colored argosies.

Sundays are also for neighborly visiting and tea. We don't deal cards or shake cocktails, and so we move in the slower set that values talk above tippling and shuffling. Much of our talk is about community problems in this changing area of subdividing and urbanization. We have a local home-owners group known as the Malibu Encinal Association, headed by Catherine Barlow. There are similar ones for Trancas Beach, Point Dume, and Zuma Canyon. All are joined in the West Malibu Community Council of which I serve as an officer. Grass roots politics. Differences of viewpoint on land, between those like us who own only the piece on which they dwell, and those owners of large tracts, to whom land is only a speculative asset.

Sunday is also the time to glean wood in the wake of the fire. Bare limbs of sumac, killed down to the root, are light and easy to cut into kindling. The new growth is already greening their bases, and after the rains the spaces between are lush with wild cucumber vines and rye grass, springing from helicopter-sown seed. We watched the "whirly birds" at work, trailing seed like smoke. Lupin and poppy make blue and gold

blankets on the bare shoulders of the hills. Brodiae, Indian paintbrush, Mariposa tulips, hairy phylos—"all the flowers of the spring meet to perfume our burying."

One could write a book about the people alone and their reasons for living in the country, starting with old-timers such as the Deckers who came long ago to ranch beyond the limits of the Rancho and to hunt wherever the deer roamed; or later ones who built along the shore in the 1930's when the Ranch was first subdivided. The Country Store at Trancas is the place to see them, and my wife has good eyes for people-watching, plus a charitable heart toward all, and someday she and I will write a novel about Malibu Man, of which there are more and more each year, alas. The longer one has lived here, the more painful it is to watch urbanization spreading like a rash.

I don't know which is sweeter, the morning when the day's work is ahead, or the evening with the prospect of sleep. After dinner I usually work by the fire, reading through the briefcase-full I brought home, preparing it for answer in the morning. I rarely write in the evening because of the difficulty in turning off my mind once it begins to work. I prefer slowly to run down. No television. No radio. The phone doesn't ring often because people don't want to make a toll call. In their thrift is our peace. My wife is in our bedroom with her own listening and reading, and assorted animals. I have long-playing records to choose from, and stretched out on the couch at the sea window, listen to music by firelight and the sound of the surf. My romantic taste ranges from Bloch, Copeland, Gershwin, and Bartok, to Scriabin, Liszt, Dvorak and Schumann, clear back to Mozart and

Bach's *Goldberg Variations*. I have experienced a revulsion for Beethoven, even his quartets, whose music, with its hammering themes and violent pianofortes, sounds coarse, after Mozart.

The latter's piano works have come to mean more to me than any other music—the concertos, sonatas and other pieces for solo instrument. In his music occurs the resolution of the discords of life. By his mastery of composition Mozart made symbols of the reconciliation of the human tragedy which, in his own life, he was unable to avert. His clarity and form and taste, permeated with his own loving nature, make Beethoven sound rough and clumsy. Beethoven for the young, Mozart for the middle aged, Bach for the old. So it sounds to me at fifty.

As I lie there in the flickering light, in the room with the golden walls and turquoise roof, this best of all music washes away the last of the day's dirt and bears me to sleep. Out the window pass the lights of the northbound trucks, red and orange, and far off gleams the jewel on Anacapa—diamond, topaz, or ruby, depending on the atmosphere.

One final turn out of doors before going to bed, giving Besa her last run. Now all is quiet save for the wash of water, and the cry of night-birds, and sometimes the swoosh of an owl. When the sea is phosphorescent, the kelp beds are milky and the breaking waves flash like neons. When the sea is high, the surf strikes the sand with hammer-blows which make the cliff shake. Sometimes fog drifts in like smoke. In the dark of the moon the purse seiners string out in a carnival of lights. The full moon's track on the water is dazzling, and once we saw an eerie lunar eclipse. Always there are planes overhead, enroute

to and from San Francisco, or Navy helicopters from Hueneme, whirling by nearly at eye level, while the Milky Way bands the sky from south to north. Lastly, the shine of city in the east— that monster which feeds on countryside, and which will eat us all in the end. But not quite yet.

Mind the long drive? Need I answer?

VIII

Twenty-nine years have passed since the preceding pages were written for a collaboration with W.W. Robinson in *The Malibu*, and nearly as many since we left seacoast for desert. The move was inevitable as "the monster" did indeed devour everything that stood in its way. It seemed better to leave than to stay and suffer the consequences. At first we spent summers back on the

coast, and then as we became inured to desert heat and our roots found nourishment in the rock and sand of the bajada, Tucson became our permanent home.

Casa Dos Vistas was leased mostly furnished, although our most precious possessions—books, records, pictures and memorabilia—went with us. Then on the 23rd of October 1978 fire finally did what it had more than once threatened to do: consumed our house and contents and many neighboring dwellings, including that of Jim and Molly Hartzell.

At least we were spared seeing it happen. Our tenants were gone for the day. There was no one to save anything of ours or theirs, although it is doubtful that it would have made any difference in the face of the wind-driven wall of fire.

Now "grass grows where the flame flowered" and the land the house occupied, no longer ours, is covered by an impressive two-story mansion. We have never returned, preferring to remember the Malibu Encinal, Place of the Live Oaks, as it was in the halcyon years. In a feverish buying and selling of land, the coast has become utterly transformed and unrecognizable. Each succeeding house, bigger and grander, takes the view of its neighbors in a kind of unbridled competition.

My collaborators on *The Malibu* have all died save Lillian Marks. When asked to update that beautiful and now rare book, I can only shake my head. Once lost, paradise can never be regained. While we lived on the coast and later, I envisioned a companion book about the back country and its comparatively few individualistic inhabitants. Most of them have now sold their land and left, and developers have bulldozed the Santa Monicas beyond recovery.

All that I wrote are these few following pages about oaks and white-tailed kites. Let them serve as my farewell to the Encinal and its once secret canyons, nay, even to California itself clear to Lassen and Shasta in the north.

୬**

THE MALIBU HILLS are full of Deckers. Ring a Glenwood number at random, they say, and the odds are a Decker will answer. One day last summer a For Sale sign appeared alongside the new road up Encinal Canyon, offering twenty-odd acres of oak-wooded, spring-fed land, and referring to a Decker family near us.

When I phoned my neighbor I learned that the owner was one of his uncles living across county in the Downey area. A call to him precipitated a lecture on local history by one of the first Deckers who came to the Malibu in the time of Mathew Keller. He ended by saying that the acreage had been sold to an outfit that intended to wildcat for oil.

"Our house was lost in the fire of '56," old Decker told me, "and we figured it was time to get out before we too got burned. Go up and have a look at what's left. At least you'll see some nice brickwork. And don't miss the sulphur spring that's never stopped flowing since we first saw it in the spring of '82. As a boy then I came over from the valley with my folks in a buckboard and we slid down the grassy hogback into the canyon, homesteaded and never left until the last burn. She was a hot one!"

On my vacation we followed Decker's suggestion. Encinal Canyon is best known to us from the lower end where we live near its confluence with the ocean. On its water we cast my mother's ashes in fulfillment of her wish that they be borne out to sea. Encinal Creek is spring-fed as are all the canyon streams in western Malibu. It flows into the Pacific the year around except at the end of a droughty season, and even then water is close to the surface.

Earlier in spring we had explored the grassy hogback described by Decker, following the oat-grown road, and there had come upon a pair of White-Tailed Kites *(Elanus leucurus),* a rodent hunting raptor tamer than most hawks, which is why hunters have pot-shot it nearly to extinction. Blue-gray on top, lighter beneath and truly white-tailed, the birds peeled off from their perch on a sycamore below the hogback and soared out on the canyon thermals. Flying gopher-traps, they are aptly called.

Later on a warm August day we returned to explore the canyon below the county road, driving along Decker's lane as far as the ruins of his house. We saw the tangled pipes, fused glass, and the great brick fireplace and chimney, reverting to wilderness as vines and chaparral made their swift recovery.

Although the canyon oaks had been badly burned, they too had revived with new growth, all but the old and weak which hadfallen and not been consumed. In the aftermath of the fire the boys and I had foraged for fallen trees, cutting them into station-wagon length to be hauled home and there sawed and split to fit our fireplace—sweet-smelling, fine-grained golden

wood, sawing smoothly, splitting easily and burning slowly in sparkless silence.

When we came to a chain across the way, we parked and walked on through the oak grove, following the sound of water over stones in the vine-hidden streambed. The sycamores had survived, and above us on the top of the highest tree we spied our kites on their hungry vigil.

Then suddenly I saw ahead an almost incredible sight rising out of the tangle of undergrowth. It was an oak of such dimensions as to stop me in my tracks, and obviously of great age. Most of the high branching limbs were gone, rotted away or burned, and yet the tree showed life in a greening of new growth along the massive trunk.

This was a Coast Live Oak *(Quercus agrifolia)*—not the Valley White Oak *(Quercus lobata)* which dwarfs its maritime cousin—and of a size never before seen in my life as a southlander. Counting on an old immunity to poison oak, I forced my way through the vines to the base of the tree. By simple measurements I gauged its bole to be six feet through, rising for a dozen feet before tapering. Clear around the trunk I circled, feeling the rough bark black with fire and age, while a blue jay in the crown challenged me with raucous scolding.

Here I imagined was once a shrine of the Oak Grove People, those acorn-eaters who preceded the tidal Chumash. Here was an altar-site fit for Druids. Such an heroic tree must have been Irminsul, sacred to the Saxons and felled by Charlemagne in the eighth century.

Awed by the discovery we pressed on along the leaf-springy

way through the grove in search of the spring described by old Decker. We might not have found it if we had not paused to listen to bird-song and then faintly heard a fall of water from a different quarter than the creekbed. Again we parted tangled vines to come upon a cemented basin into which water was flowing steadily from a pipe. Fresh and cold and not unpleasantly sulphured, the spring ran despite the drought that had shrunk the other sweetwater sources of Encinal Creek.

Since 1882 Decker had vouched for its flow. Since forever, I thought, this source of life and health had made the encinal a sacred grove. Even our little dog Besa was subdued as we made our way back to the car and left the canyon.

One winter I went up Lechuza Canyon to the west of Encinal Canyon to saw up a sycamore felled by the great fire of '56. It was the day when the first rain came "with love in its touches." How cool it felt on my bare back, how good it sounded on the leaves!

I worked on in the soft rain until I had the station wagon loaded, then followed a deer path to the creek which had maintained its flow despite the autumnal drought. Squatting down I drank and then gathered a mess of watercress from the surface of the steam.

Later at ebb tide we went to the beach to get our supper off the rocks. Prying abalones from the reef is only half the labor required: the other end of the mollusk is almost as firmly fastened to the shell. Living off the land and sea takes strong hands.

After our candlelight-and-Mozart meal before the fire, I re-

called another old oak seen the week before on our Christmas visit to Fay's parents at Los Molinos, far up the Sacramento River valley in the lee of Lassen and sight of Shasta.

This was an oak I had read about but never seen—the Sir Joseph Hooker oak at Chico, named by Annie Bidwell in 1853 for the English botanist, a deciduous Valley White Oak estimated to be a thousand years old. Hooker himself saw it in 1877 in company with Professor Asa Gray of Harvard and pronounced it to be the largest oak in the world, although Peattie says that it is not.

Certainly it is the biggest oak I have ever seen; and seen in winter, its few remaining golden leaves affording a view of the tree's skeleton, it was a sight not possible in summer's full leaf. One hundred ten feet high, its trunk eight feet in diameter at the base, the tree accommodates two thousand people in its pool of shade. Peattie gives these figures in his *Natural History of Western Trees,* a volume illustrated from wood engravings by Paul Landacre.

When on a windy Christmas Day we sought it out in the deserted park east of Chico, the Hooker Oak stood alone, equally majestic with the two great snow-covered mountains in the north and northeast. Tree surgeons have cared for it, cabling the crown branches and supporting the down-swept limbs on concrete stands. *Quercus lobata* is useless except for firewood. It rots in the ground, making it worthless for fence posts. Although the wood is hard, it is also brittle. Early settlers called it Mush Oak.

And yet the Hooker Oak has stood for millennium and with

the care given it, will probably stand for many more years. We lingered under the great tree, bundled against the biting cold and gathered fallen acorns. I vowed to plant one back home among the oaks in Encinal Canyon. In vain. The two varieties will grow together, but only in *Lobata's* domain. *Agrifolia* can survive without seafog; *Lobata* can't stand it.

Still it was a nice thought. Remember what Sterne said? The only truly important things a man can do are get a child, build a house, write a book, and plant a tree.

I was too optimistic in believing that the Hooker Oak would stand for years to come. In spite of all that was done to ensure its survival, the ancient tree began to break up in the 1970s in the unusually fierce storms that swept the valley. First its symmetry was lost when half the tree split off in one storm. That was a sad sight. I never returned to see the remaining stages of dismemberment.

ONE SUMMER in Malibu a few years before the final fire, I drove a friend up Encinal Canyon to see the great live oak. I hadn't been back in many years. New roads and buildings scarred the canyon. Brush and vines had run wild, making it hard to get my bearings. The road to the spring was barred by a locked gate.

We left the Scout and reconnoitered. I kept looking in vain for where I had seen the great trunk rising from the undergrowth. At last I perceived what what looked like a fallen elephant. Pressing through the tangle we came on the shattered remains of the old giant. Storm had finally brought it down as it

had the Hooker Oak, and there it sprawled in pieces, proof that I had not exaggerated its girth.

LET ME END this somber report on fallen titans with a happier note on *Elanus leucurus.* It is occasioned by a story in the *Los Angeles Times,* headed "White-Tailed Kite Comes Soaring Back." Although my clipping is undated, the article appeared some time during the 1970s. It tells of how the kites have found food and security along the grassy shoulders and broad open-center dividers of Southern California's freeways and fenced flood control channels. Because hunters are barred from these areas, the rodent- and insect-feeding birds have thrived.

As they soar and glide they look like seagulls until they pause to flutter, then drop with out-stretched talons on their prey. Perched on a freeway fence or power line, they show the snowy white chest and tail, the black patches on the shoulders, and the black mask-like marks across the fierce eyes. If you should look for them, also keep your eyes on the road if you too are to survive!

In 1913 while living in London, Mary Austin wrote the text for a book of paintings of California. After lamenting the passage of the land she first knew from her girlhood arrival in the 1880s, she ended with these words: "In two or three generations, when towns have taken on the tone of time, and the courageous wild has re-established itself in by-lanes and corners, a writer may be born, instinctively at one with his

natural environment, and so able to give satisfying expression
to that wholeness."

   Perhaps that is why I continue to write, and even to hope.

Tucson
Bajada of the
Santa Catalinas